THE GROUND IS SHAKING!

WHAT HAPPENS DURING AN EARTHQUAKE?

GEOLOGY FOR BEGINNERS

Children's Geology Books

Speedy Publishing LLC
40 E. Main St. #1156
Newark, DE 19711
www.speedypublishing.com

Have you ever experienced an earthquake? The resulting shaking of the Earth is caused by two big blocks suddenly slipping against one another. Read further to learn more about what causes them, where they occur, and how they are measured.

Sichuan earthquake – China.

WHAT IS AN EARTHQUAKE?

An earthquake occurs once two areas of the Earth slip suddenly past each other. The fault plane or fault is the area where they slip against each other. The hypocenter is the location that is below the surface where it started, and the area directly on the surface above it is known as the epicenter. This is where the earthquake is at its strongest.

Occasionally you might experience a fore-shock, which is a smaller earthquake prior to the larger one, occurring in the same location. Scientists are not able to distinguish a foreshock until the larger earthquake occurs. The larger quake is referred to as the mainshock, which always will be followed by aftershocks. As with the foreshock, the aftershock will always occur at the same location as the mainshock.

Dependent upon the size of the mainshock, its possible for the aftershocks to continue for days, weeks, months and years following the mainshock.

Landscape view of jagged fault line.

WHAT CAUSES AN EARTHQUAKE?

The Earth consists of four layers; the crust, the mantle, the outer core and the inner core. The thin skin located on our planet's surface consists of the top of the mantle and crust. However, the skin consists of several pieces, similar to a puzzle. In addition, these pieces continue to move, slipping past each other and bumping against each other.

These pieces are known as tectonic plates, with their edges being the plate boundaries. These boundaries consist of several faults, with most earthquakes occurring on the faults. The plates' edges are rough causing them to get stuck as the remaining plate continues to move. Once the plate has shifted far enough, the edges will release on one of these faults, causing the earthquake.

MOVEMENT OF TECTONIC PLATES

The plates' movement is evident mostly at the boundaries between them. The three different types are listed below:

Convergent Boundaries – This is when two plates push themselves together. Occasionally, one will move underneath the other one, which is known as subduction. Although they move slowly, these boundaries can be an area of activity such as formation of volcanoes and mountains, as well high activity for earthquakes.

Convergent Plate Boundary.

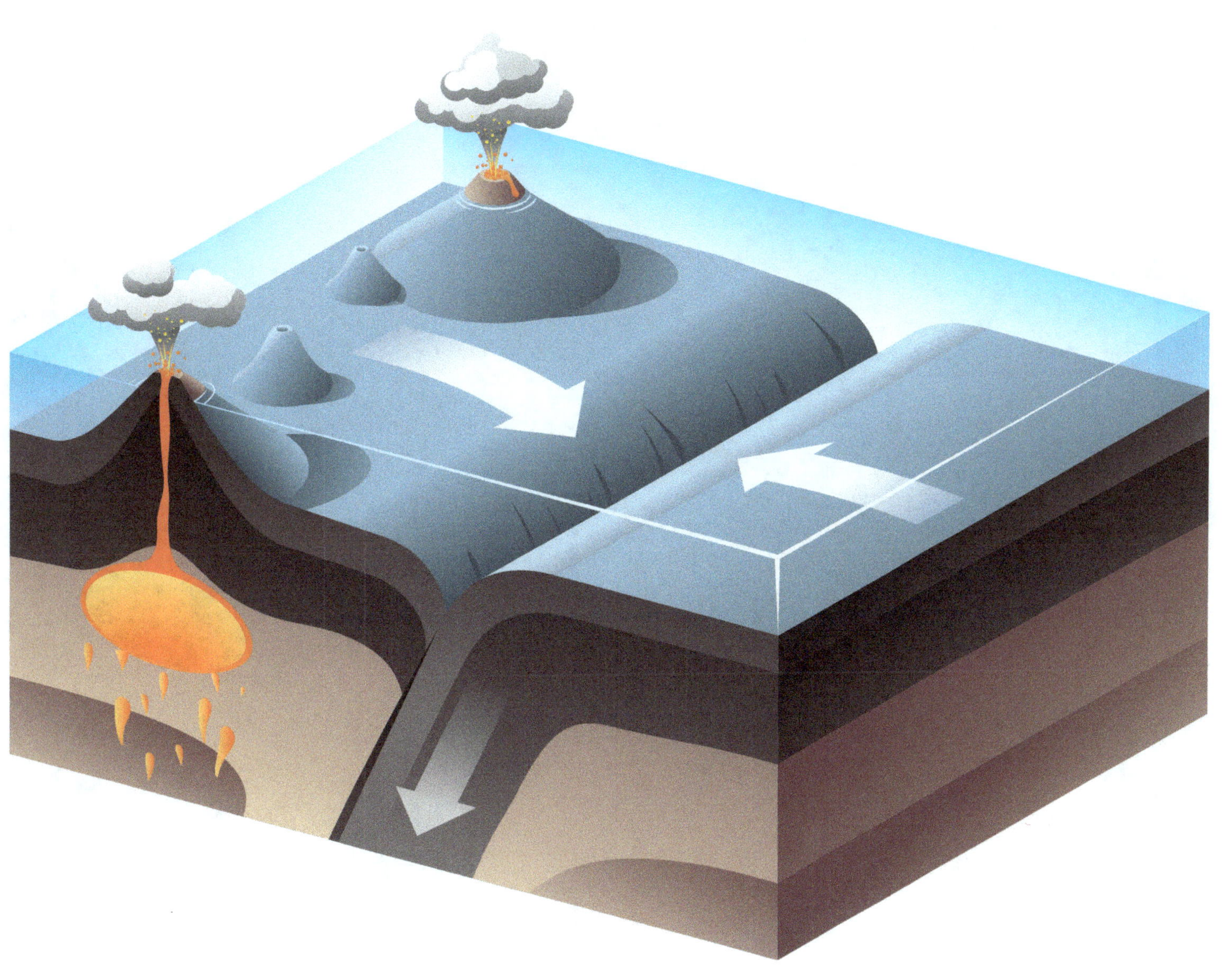

Divergent Boundaries – This occurs when one plate is pushed away from the other one, and this area is known as a rift. Magma then forms new land by pushing up and cooling as it comes to the surface.

Divergent Plate Boundary.

Transform Boundaries – This is where the two plates slip past one another. These are often referred to as faults and are known to be places where earthquakes occur often.

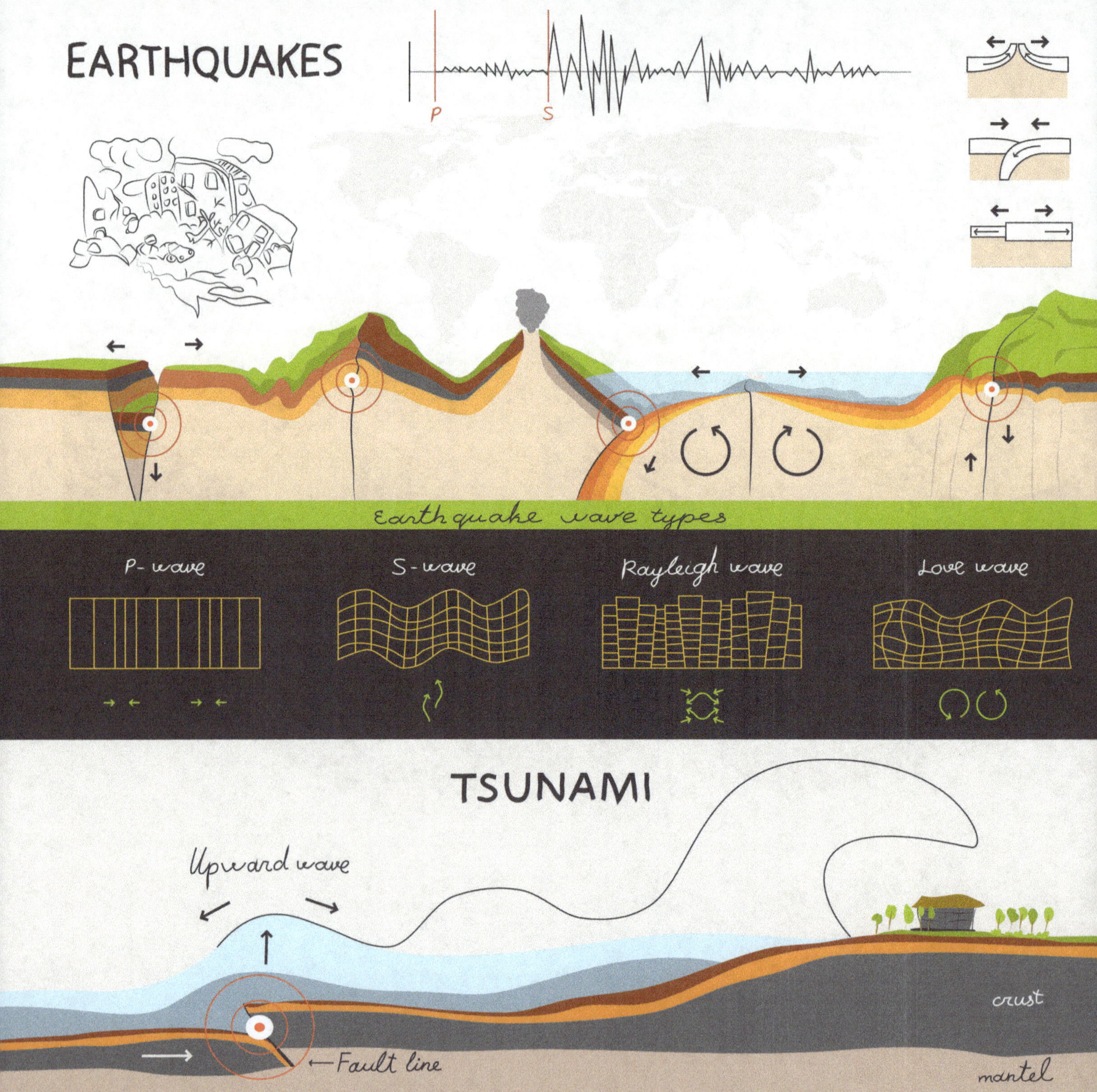

EARTHQUAKES
P
S
Earthquake wave types
P-wave
S-wave
Rayleigh wave
Love wave
TSUNAMI
Upward wave
Fault line
crust
mantel

WHAT IS A SEISMIC WAVE?

The shock waves resulting from an earthquake travelling through the ground are known as seismic waves. These waves are more powerful at the quake's center, but travel through much of our planet and return back to the surface. They travel quickly, 20 times the speed of sound.

These waves are used by scientists for measuring the size of an earthquake. The device they use to measure the wave's size is known as a seismograph, and the wave's size is known as its magnitude.

Earthquake and Tsunami Info-graphics.

In order to find out the earthquake's strength, scientists use an *MMS – Moment Magnitude Scale,* which was previously known as the Richter scale. The larger the earthquake, the greater the MMS number. Typically, a quake has to be at least 3 on the MMS meter for you to notice it. Listed below are examples of what can occur depending on the scale number:

4.0 – Your house might shake similar to a big truck going by. This might not be noticed by some people.

Fault.

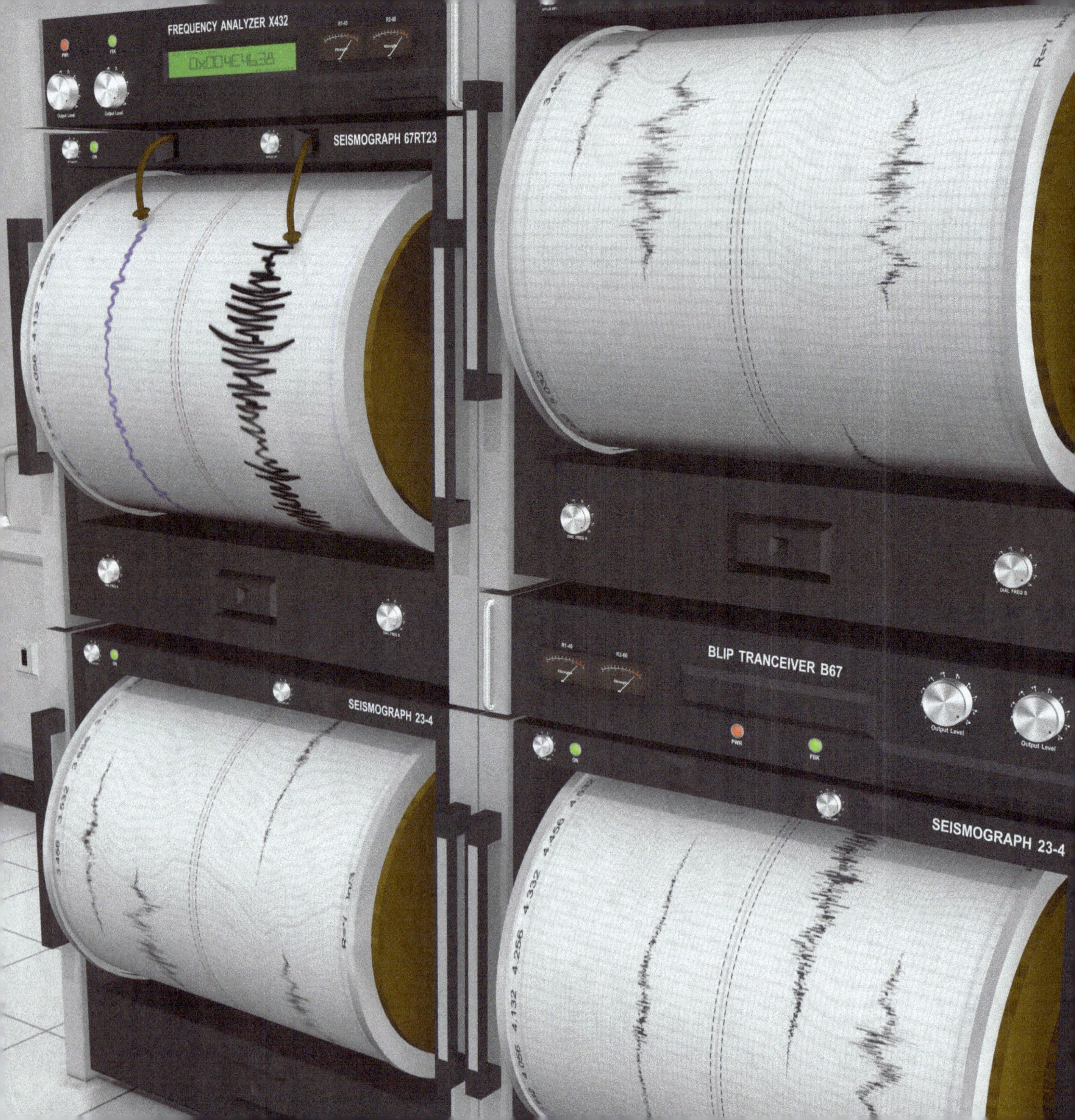

FREQUENCY ANALYZER X432
0x004E4b38
SEISMOGRAPH 67RT23
SEISMOGRAPH 23-4
BLIP TRANCEIVER B67
SEISMOGRAPH 23-4
PWR
FBK
Output Level
Output Level
ON
R1-60
R2-60

6.0 – Items may fall from their shelves. Some walls in houses might crack and windows might break. Anyone near the center of the quake will notice this one.

7.0 – Weaker and older buildings will fall and bridges and street will get cracks in them.

8.0 – Several bridges and buildings will come down. The Earth will get large cracks in it.

9.0 and up – Whole towns and cities be flattened with a great amount of damage resulting.

What Are The Largest Earthquakes In History?

- Valdivia, Chile, occurring on May 22, 1960, with a magnitude of 9.5.

- Sumatra, Indonesia, occurring on December 26, 2004, with a magnitude of 9.3.

- Prince William Sound, Alaska, USA, occurring on March 27, 1964, with a magnitude of 9.2

- Kamchatka, USSR, occurring on November 4, 1952, with a magnitude of 9.0.

- Arica, Chile, occurring on August 13, 1868, with a magnitude of 9.0.

Fissures near Jerocarne in Calabria.

- Cascadia subduction zone, Canada and USA, occurring on January 26, 1700, with a magnitude of 9.0.

- Maule, Chile, occurring on February 27, 2010, with a magnitude of 8.8.

- Ecuador and Colombia, occurring on January 31, 1906, with a magnitude of 8.8.

- Sumatra, Indonesia, occurring on November 25, 1833, with a magnitude of 8.8.

The earthquake of Lisbon.

- Rat Islands, Alaska, USA, occurring on February 4, 1965, with a magnitude of 8.7.

- Lisbon, Portugal, occurring on November 1, 1755, with a magnitude of 8.7.

- Valparaiso, Chile, occurring on July 8, 1730, with a magnitude of 8.7.

The Great East Japan Earthquake.

Seismograph and earthquake.

HOW ARE SCIENTISTS ABLE TO TELL WHERE AN EARTHQUAKE OCCURRED?

Seismograms are helpful in locating where the earthquake occurred, using the P and S waves. These waves shake the ground each in a different way as they move through it. S waves are slower than P waves, which allows us to find the location of the quake.

Think of the P and S waves as thunder and lightning. Since light travels at a faster speed than sound does, you will observe the lightning prior to hearing the thunder. The closer you are to the lightning, the quicker you will hear the thunder after seeing the lightning. Sometimes you can even count several seconds after the lightning before you hear the thunder.

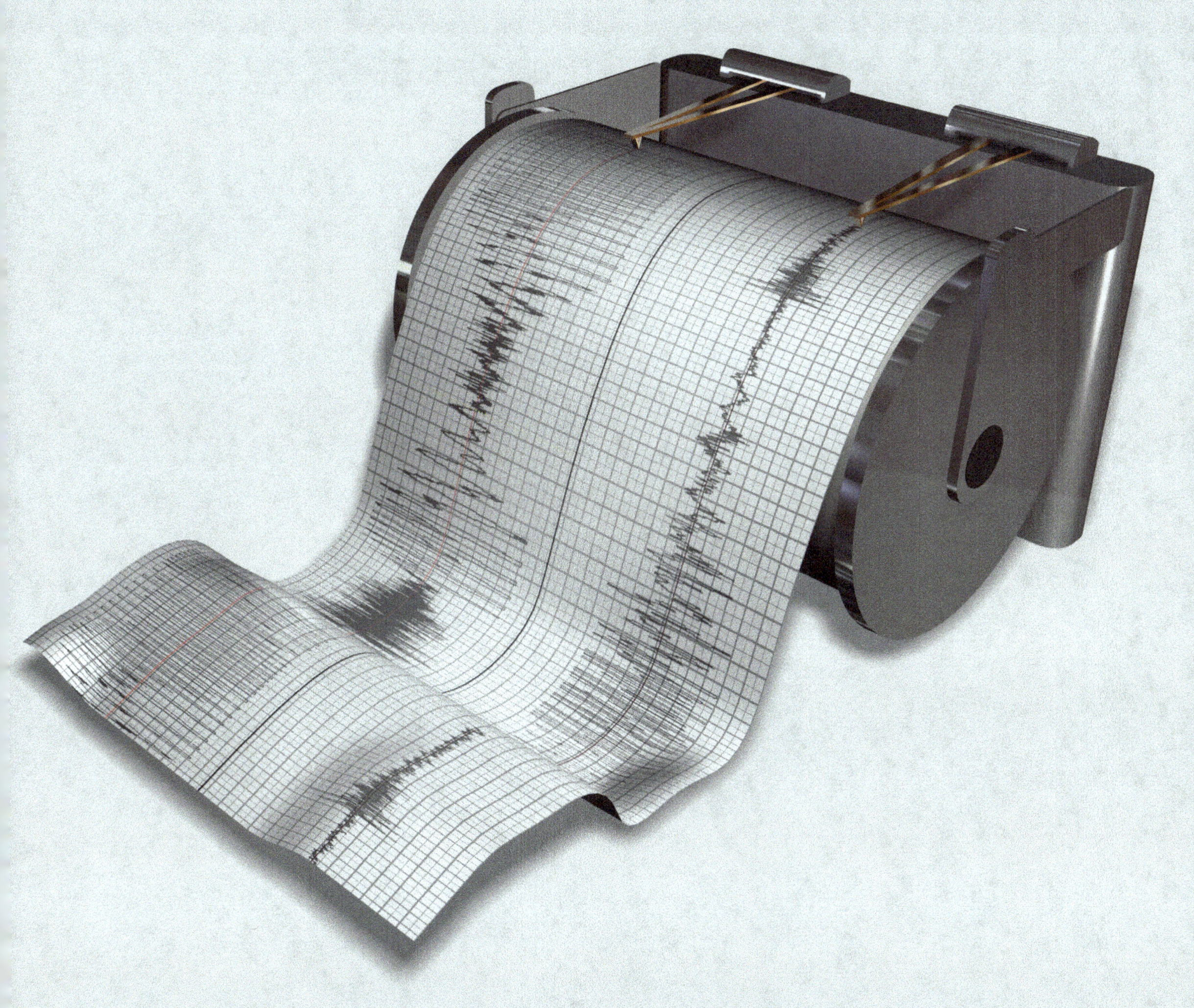

The P waves are similar to the lightning, and the S waves are similar to the thunder. Since the P waves move faster, they shake the ground first. After you feel the P waves, the S waves will follow and will also cause the ground to shake. If you are located close to the quake, both waves will follow one another quickly, but if you are farther away, more time will elapse between the two waves.

By analyzing the time between the P and S waves on the seismogram recorded on the seismograph, the scientists can detect the distance between the earthquake and that location. They are not able to tell what direction the quake was from the seismograph, only the distance.

If the scientists draw a circle on a map surrounding the station of the circle's radius, this is determined to be the distance to the quake, and they realize that the earthquake is located in the circle somewhere, but where?

Search and rescue after an earthquake.

They will then use triangulation, a method for determining where exactly it is located. It is referred to as triangulation since it needs three seismographs for locating the earthquake, and a triangle consists of three sides. When a circle is drawn on the map surrounding three seismographs, the distance is where the radius of each station to the earthquake, and where they intersect is considered to be the epicenter!

Split in earth.

Damaged Road.

CAN EARTHQUAKES BE PREDICTED?

Unfortunately, no they cannot be predicted and will probably never be able to be predicted. Scientists have tried several ways of predicting earthquakes, but have not been successful. On any one fault, they know there can be a quake, but have no way to tell when it might happen.

To date, scientists are unable to tell if weather affects an occurrence, or if people or animals know when one is about to strike.

Earthquake damaged buildings.

Apocalyptic scene tsunami.

WHAT IS A TSUNAMI?

A tsunami is a powerful and large ocean wave that gets bigger as it reaches the shoreline. They have the ability to cause a great amount of damage as they come inland, destroying homes and flooding cities.

A tsunami is caused by a displacement of water that is very large. Think about sitting in the bathtub and once you move around, a large wave occurs. This is what occurs in the ocean as a big amount of water suddenly moves.

TSUNAMI

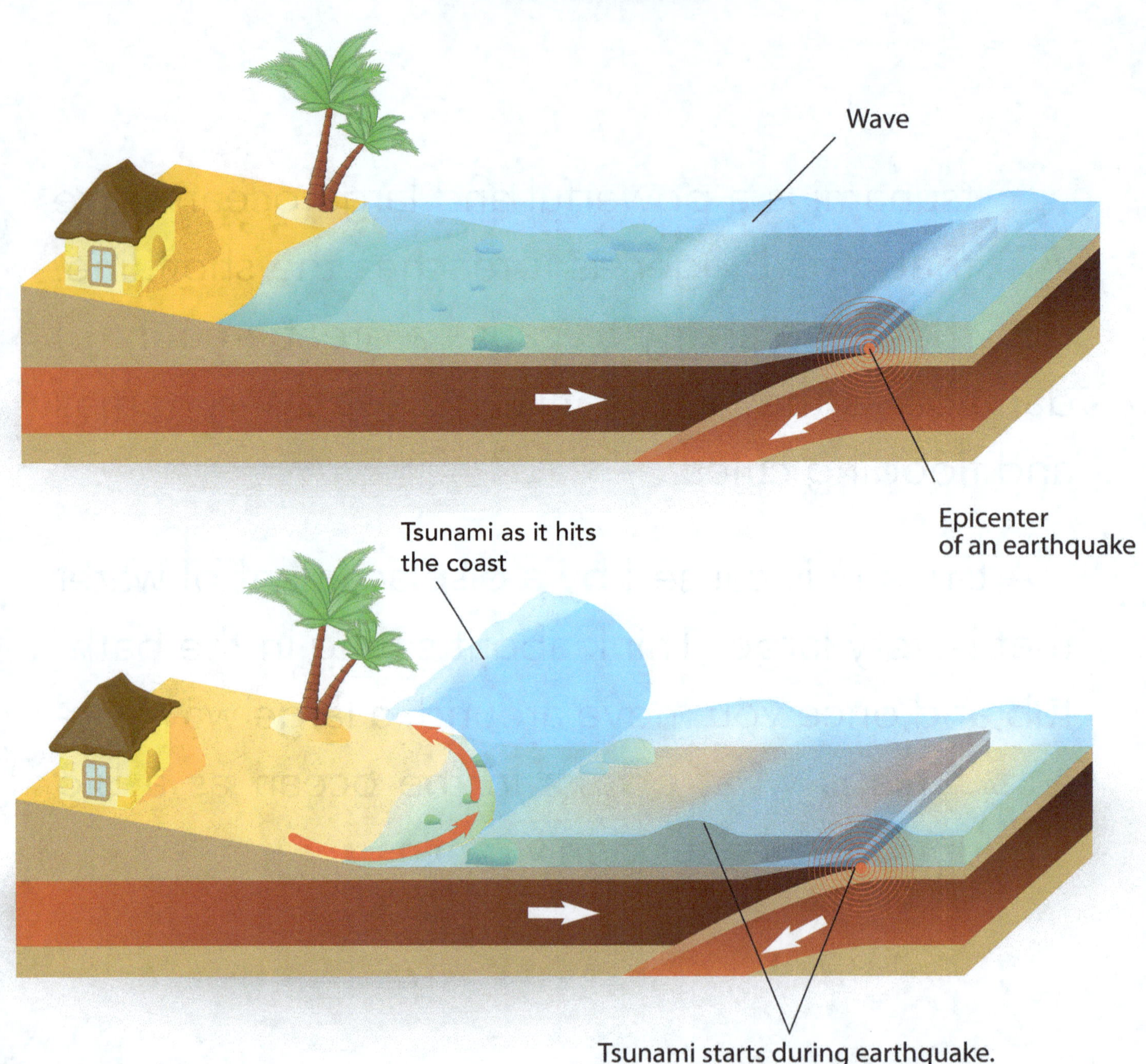

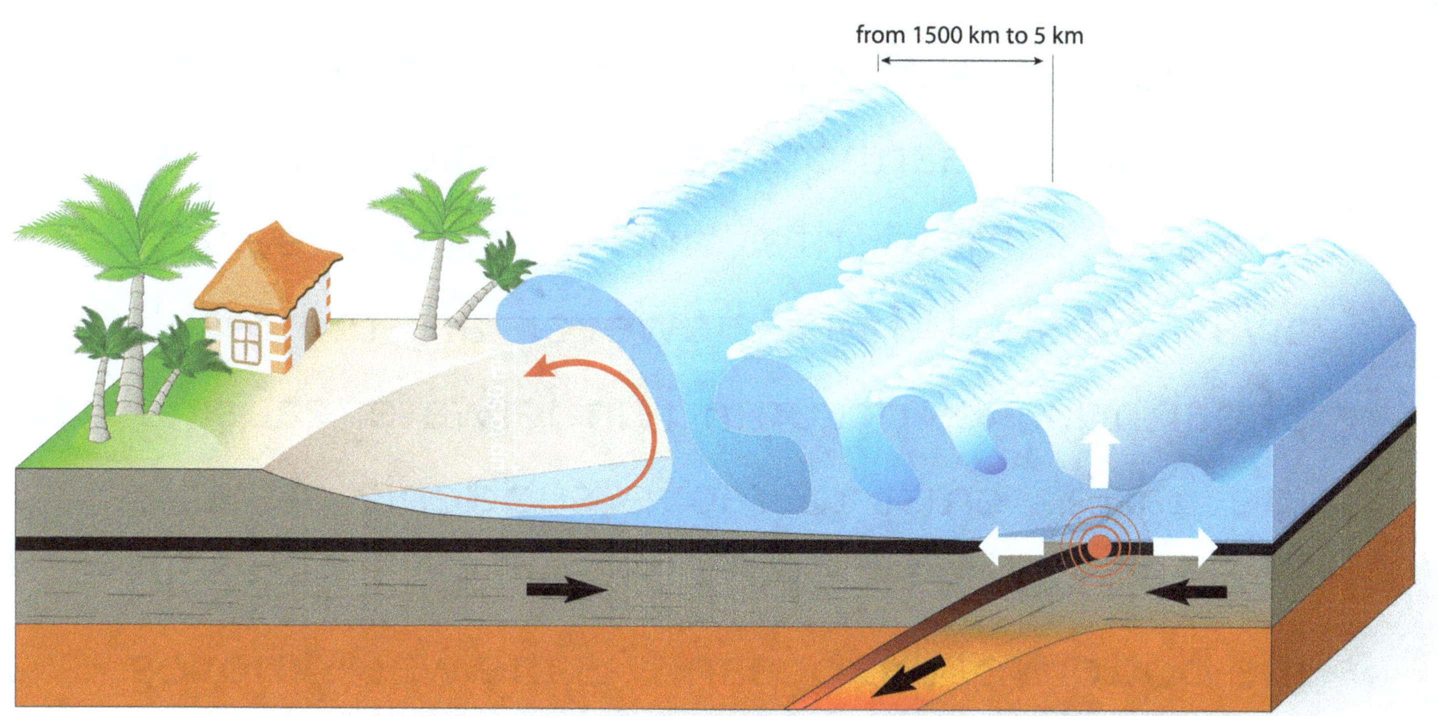
from 1500 km to 5 km

Several events can cause this movement, including earthquakes, volcanic eruptions, landslides, meteorites and glaciers breaking away. Most of them, however, are the result of earthquakes occurring underwater causing the Earth's crust to move suddenly. As this occurs underwater, large gaps can appear on the bottom of the ocean. As the water moves to fill the gap, the tsunami is created.

Now that you have learned some basic information about earthquakes, you can find additional information by going to your local library, researching the internet, and asking questions of your teachers, family, and friends.

Visit

BABY PROFESSOR
EDUCATION KIDS

www.BabyProfessorBooks.com
to download Free Baby Professor eBooks
and view our catalog of new and exciting
Children's Books